A Robbie Reader

Class Trip
BOSTON

Patrice Sherman

COOK MEMORIAL LIBRARY
413 N. MILWAUKEE AVE.
LIBERTYVILLE, ILLINOIS 60048

Mitchell Lane
PUBLISHERS

P.O. Box 196
Hockessin, Delaware 19707
Visit us on the web: www.mitchelllane.com
Comments? email us: mitchelllane@mitchelllane.com

Mitchell Lane

PUBLISHERS

Class Trip

Boston • New York City • Philadelphia
San Antonio • San Diego
Washington, DC

Copyright © 2010 by Mitchell Lane Publishers

All rights reserved. No part of this book may be reproduced without written permission from the publisher. Printed and bound in the United States of America.

PUBLISHER'S NOTE: The facts on which the story in this book is based have been thoroughly researched. Documentation of such research can be found on page 46. While every possible effort has been made to ensure accuracy, the publisher will not assume liability for damages caused by inaccuracies in the data, and makes no warranty on the accuracy of the information contained herein.

Printing   1   2   3   4   5   6   7   8   9

Library of Congress
Cataloging-in-Publication Data
Sherman, Patrice.
   Class trip Boston / by Patrice Sherman.
       p. cm. — (Robbie reader, class trip)
   Includes bibliographical references and index.
   ISBN 978-1-58415-806-6 (library bound)
   1. Boston (Mass.)—Juvenile literature. 2. School field trips—Massachusetts—Boston—Juvenile literature. I. Title.
   F73.33.S54 2010
   974.4'61—dc22
                                                    2009001107

                                                    PLB

CONTENTS

BOSTON

Acorn Street in Beacon Hill, one of Boston's oldest neighborhoods, is still paved with cobblestones that were laid in the early eighteenth century. Many of the stones came from England, where they had been loaded onto sailing ships as ballast to keep the vessels upright in the water. Top right: Abigail Adams

Chapter 1

The Class Trip to Boston Committee

Hi! My name is Abby. That's short for Abigail. Did you know that Abigail Adams, the second First Lady of the United States, and her husband, President John Adams, came from Boston? I love history. Can't you tell? It's my favorite subject. I'm in the fourth grade at the Katherine Lee Bates Elementary School in Wellesley, Massachusetts, less than 20 miles from Boston.

When our teacher, Ms. Park, told us we were taking a class trip to Boston, you can bet I was excited. And when she asked for volunteers to help prepare a report about the city and make a list of places we could visit, my hand shot right up. A lot of my friends volunteered too, so we decided to form the Fourth Grade Class Trip to Boston Committee and meet right after school. I was elected chairperson unanimously (yoo-NAA-nuh-mus-lee). That means everybody voted for me.

That's when all my problems began. Let me explain.

Luther, a white Bengal tiger, arrived at the Franklin Park Zoo in 2006 when he was about a year old. One of the zoo's most popular residents, he is part of the Tiger Tales exhibit.

I immediately started to write down all the historic sites in Boston. There's, oh, maybe about five hundred of them. At least. Then my friend Jen, who loves sports, said, "We have to tell everybody about Boston's great teams. The Red Sox, the Celtics, the Bruins, and the New England Patriots."

"Don't forget the Museum of Fine Arts," added Carl, who spends all his time drawing and is going to be a great artist someday.

"And the Boston Symphony," Lisa, our class chorus leader, piped up.

"And the Museum of Science," said Jill, the future scientist.

"And the Franklin Park Zoo," insisted Mike, who's crazy about animals and wants to be a veterinarian, which is an animal doctor, when he grows up.

Everybody had a different idea of what was most important. Stan, who's into sailing, said we had to include Boston Harbor and all the harbor islands you could visit during the summer.

Cindy asked, "What about ice-skating on Frog Pond on Boston **C o m m o n** during the winter?"

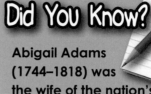

Did You Know?

Abigail Adams (1744–1818) was the wife of the nation's second president. She was known for her wit, intelligence, and strong support of women's rights. The many letters she wrote to her husband are treasured as a unique source of American history.

John Adams (1735–1826) was born in Braintree, just south of Boston. He attended Harvard and later became a lawyer. He served as George Washington's vice president for eight years, and then as president from 1797 to 1801.

WELCOME
TO THE BOSTON COMMON
FROG POND
SKATING RINK
RATES
CHILDREN
(13 AND UNDER)
FREE ADMISSION
$5.00 SKATE RENTAL
ADULTS
$4.00 ADMISSION (PLUS)
$8.00 SKATE RENTAL ($12.00 TOTAL)
$1.00 Locker Rental
$5.00 Skate Sharpening
(SALES STOP 30 MINUTES BEFORE CLOSING)
$20.00 minimum for all credit cards.
Absolutely No Refunds.
Bathrooms are for Patrons Only

And Lou and Lee, the twins, reminded us that Faneuil (FAN-yul) Hall Marketplace is the most fabulous place for lunch. You can find everything there, from pizza to bagels to burritos to egg rolls, Indian curry,

Japanese soba noodles, homemade ice cream, and, of course, Boston baked beans. That made us all hungry, so we went over to my house for a snack.

My dad was home, and when he found out what we were doing, he said, "Did you know that the greater Boston area has over thirty colleges and universities? People come from all over the world to study there. That's something you can add to your report."

"Thanks, Dad." I groaned. I felt like my head was going to explode.

Even after they left, my friends kept calling and texting with suggestions. We couldn't agree on anything.

When I got to school the next day, I told Ms. Park she'd have to call our class trip off.

"Why?" She looked alarmed.

Did You Know?

Katherine Lee Bates

Abby's elementary school is named for Katherine Lee Bates (1859–1929), who wrote the words to the song "America the Beautiful." They were published by the *Boston Evening Transcript* in 1904. She lived near Boston, in Wellesley and Newton, Massachusetts.

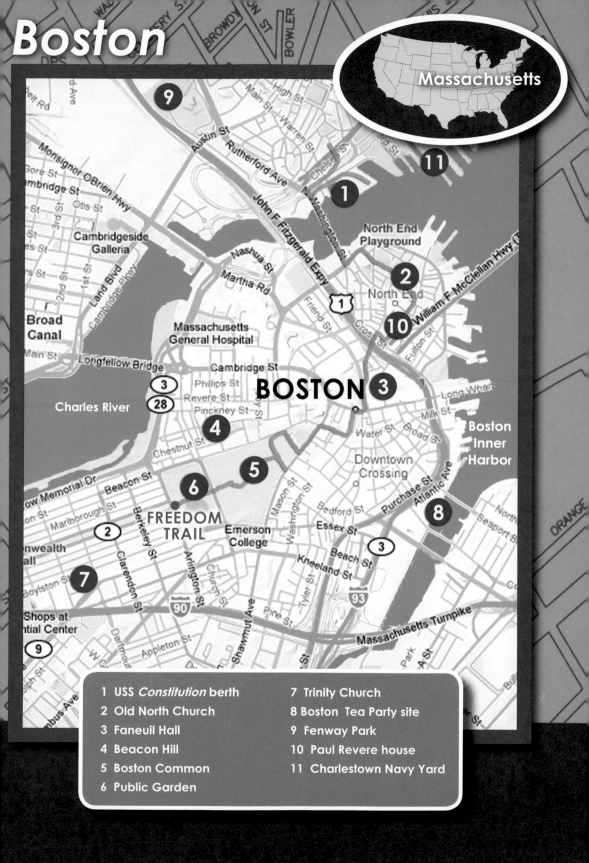

Boston

Massachusetts

BROWDY ST
BOWLER

9

Austin St
Rutherford Ave
John F Fitzgerald Expy

Main St
High St
Warren St

1

N Washington St
Chelsea St

11

Monsignor OBrien Hwy
Cambridge St
Otis St

Nashua St
Martha Rd

North End
Playground

North End

2

William F McClellan Hwy

Cambridgeside
Galleria

Friend St

1

10

Broad
Canal

Massachusetts
General Hospital

Fulton St

Main St

Longfellow Bridge

Cambridge St

BOSTON

3

Long Wharf

Charles River

3
28

Phillips St
Revere St
Pinckney St

Milk St

Boston
Inner
Harbor

4

Chestnut St

Water St
Broad St

Beacon St

5

Downtown
Crossing

Purchase St
Atlantic Ave

Marlborough St

6

Mason St
Washington St

Bedford St

FREEDOM
TRAIL

Emerson
College

Essex St

8

onwealth
all

2

Berkeley St
Clarendon St

Beach St
Kneeland St

3

7

Boylston St

Arlington St
Church St

Tyler St

93

Shops at
tial Center

90

Appleton St

Shawmut Ave
Pine St

Massachusetts Turnpike

9

Dartmouth

W C

bus Ave

A St

1 USS *Constitution* berth
2 Old North Church
3 Faneuil Hall
4 Beacon Hill
5 Boston Common
6 Public Garden

7 Trinity Church
8 Boston Tea Party site
9 Fenway Park
10 Paul Revere house
11 Charlestown Navy Yard

"Because," I explained, "we'll all be in fifth grade by the time we finish this report."

She laughed. "Maybe you need a little help."

We got the committee together and she looked over our list. "First things first," she told us. "Where's Boston?"

Where's Boston? We all stared at each other.

"It's in Massachusetts."

"New England."

"The United States."

"North America."

"We need a map!" I said.

"That's right," Ms. Park replied.

We did some research and found some maps. Boston is on the northeast coast of the United States in the state of Massachusetts. It's about halfway up the state, right on the Atlantic Ocean.

Then Ms. Park helped us focus on some of the things we could all agree on. We couldn't put everything about Boston in our report, but we could add a list of books and web sites at the end, where kids could find more information. We could also put together a list of important facts and **statistics** (stuh-TIS-tiks) to use as a quick way of learning about Boston.

As the chairperson of the Trip to Boston Committee (which was back in business), I suggested we start with a little history.

Everyone thought that was a good idea.

So here we go. Let's step into Boston's time machine.

Old Ironsides sails in Boston Harbor. Boston is rich in history, and visitors get a taste of old and new as they tour the city.

BOSTON

Boston Public Garden is across Charles Street from Boston Common. The garden includes the four-acre pond Bostonians call the lagoon. Winding paths around the lagoon are shaded by weeping willows and other trees. Top right: Park Street Subway Station

Chapter 2

Boston's Time Machine: A Quick Trip Through History

Why is Boston like a time machine? Because every place you go, you're surrounded by history. Even riding the subway into Boston is historic. Boston has the oldest subway system in the United States. The first tunnel, which was located under Tremont Street, opened in 1897. Back then, sparks really flew. All the subway cars had open windows, and ladies wearing big fancy hats had to make sure they didn't catch on fire. Today, the subway is a lot safer, and still a great way to get to and around the city.

If you get off the train at Park Street Station and go straight up to street level, you'll find yourself standing on the edge of Boston Common, the first public park in America. In 1634, the Puritans set aside this land for grazing cows and sheep. You won't see any farm animals there now, though you may see people walking their dogs.

The **Puritans** arrived from England in 1630, landing on a small **peninsula** (peh-NIN-suh-luh) called **Shawmut** by the Massachusett, a group of people from the Wampanoag (wom-puh-NOH-ug) tribe who were already living there. (Can you guess how the state got its name?) Boston got its name from the town in England (Boston!) where many of the Puritans had lived.

Education was important to the Puritans. In 1635, they scored another first by founding Boston Latin School, the first public school in America. Today, it is one of Boston's best and toughest high schools. And the students still take Latin!

Did You Know?

The Wampanoag are a Native American tribe from southeastern New England. They were among first residents of the Boston area, and they welcomed the Puritans in 1630. Today, the Wampanoag people number just over 2,000. Many live on the island of Martha's Vineyard and in the town of Mashpee on Cape Cod.

Brewing Up Trouble: The Boston Tea Party

Because of its large harbor, Boston soon became one of the busiest trading ports in the British colonies. Britain wanted to keep tight control over this trade, so it passed many laws governing what people could buy and sell and how much the goods should cost. The colonists resented these laws, especially the taxes they felt made British companies rich and kept colonial companies poor. They plotted a protest against the tax laws. On the night of December 16, 1773, a group

One hundred and sixteen colonists are known to have participated in the Boston Tea Party. Their act of protest sparked groups in other colonies to stage similar protests against British taxes.

of Boston men disguised as Native Americans snuck onto a British merchant vessel and threw over 90,000 pounds of tea into Boston Harbor. That's a lot of tea. And it brewed a lot of trouble.

Ready in a Minute: The Minutemen Take On the British
Britain responded to the colonial protest by sending troops to enforce the king's laws. In turn, the colonists organized volunteer **militias** to defend themselves. Tension started to boil.

Two years after the Tea Party, British troops marched on the towns of Lexington and Concord to seize the rebels' supplies. Unknown to them, however, someone else was headed that way too. On April 19, 1775, Paul Revere, a Boston silversmith, took one of the most famous rides in American history. Mounted on a borrowed horse, he rode 20 miles from Boston to Concord to warn the residents that the British were coming. By dawn, the **Minutemen** were ready and waiting on the Lexington Town Green. Shots rang out. The first battle of the Revolutionary War had begun.

Paul Revere was not the only rider on April 18, 1775. William Dawes of Boston's militia rode to Concord via another route. The two men met near Lexington and were joined by Dr. Samuel Prescott. Prescott woke his brother Abel, who spread the alarm too.

Freedom for All: Boston and the Civil War

The United States won its independence from Britain in 1783. Unfortunately, most African Americans couldn't enjoy the new freedom. They were slaves. Massachusetts, though, officially ended slavery within the state in 1783. Many people began to believe that slavery should be outlawed in every state. William Lloyd Garrison, a leading **abolitionist** (aa-buh-LIH-shuh-nist) in Boston, began publishing his newspaper, *The Liberator,* in 1831. Over the next thirty years, his paper made Boston a center of the antislavery movement. African American leaders Frederick Douglass and Sojourner Truth spoke to crowds at Faneuil Hall calling for the end of slavery.

During the Civil War, Massachusetts organized one of the first African American regiments, the 54th Massachusetts Volunteer Infantry. Under the command of Colonel Robert Gould Shaw, a white officer from Boston, the soldiers of the 54th Regiment fought at the Battle of Fort Wagner in South Carolina. Sergeant William Harvey Carney stormed the enemy ramparts carrying the flag. "It never touched the ground," he said later. For his bravery, he was awarded the Medal of Honor in 1900.

William Harvey Carney

The memorial to the 54th Massachusetts Volunteer Infantry is made of bronze and took fourteen years to complete. Philosopher William James, who spoke at the dedication ceremony in 1897, called the soldiers "champions of a better day for man."

A memorial to the 54th Regiment is located on Boston Common and forms part of the city's African American Heritage Trail.

Beantown Becomes Boomtown: Triple-Deckers and an Emerald Necklace

After the Civil War, **immigrants** (IH-mih-grints) from all over the world started pouring into Boston. Irishmen, Italians, Poles, Lithuanians, Greeks, Syrians, Jews from Eastern Europe, and African Americans from the southern United States all contributed to the city's growth. Between 1870 and 1920, Boston's population tripled, from 250,000 people to over 750,000. Many of these new residents moved into **triple-deckers**, three-story wooden apartment buildings that housed a family on each floor. Even today, Bostonians love their triple-deckers, and you can find many beautifully preserved examples in neighborhoods like Dorchester, Jamaica Plain, Roslindale, and Roxbury.

Frederick Law Olmsted

The city also acquired a living Emerald Necklace. Planned by landscape architect Frederick Law Olmsted, the "jewels" in this necklace aren't stones but a series of parks stretching across the city. These parks include Boston Common, the Public Garden, the Charles River Esplanade, the Fenway, and Franklin Park, home of the Franklin Park Zoo.

Rosie the Riveter Rolls Up Her Sleeves: The Charlestown Navy Yard in World War II

Established in 1800, the Charlestown Navy Yard served as a U.S. Naval Base for 174 years. It was the home of the USS *Constitution*, a ship so tough it became known as Old Ironsides for its ability to withstand enemy cannonballs during the War of 1812. The Yard constructed ships for the Union forces during the Civil

War and also manufactured hundreds of miles of rope in its steam-powered **ropewalk**.

It was World War II, however, that spurred record production. From 1941 to 1945, over 50,000 people, including 8,500 women, worked in the shipyard. They built 156 new vessels and repaired over 3,200 others damaged in combat. Though some of the women held office jobs, most of them worked on the assembly line alongside the men, welding and riveting the aircraft carriers and destroyers that would help the United States and its allies win the war.

Today the Navy Yard is a National Historic Site. On display are both Old Ironsides and the USS *Cassin Young*, a destroyer from World War II.

Did You Know?

Rosie the Riveter was a nickname given to women who worked in heavy industry during World War II. Over 8,500 "Rosies" helped build and repair ships in Boston's Charlestown Navy Yard.

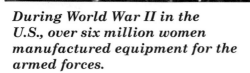

During World War II in the U.S., over six million women manufactured equipment for the armed forces.

Digging Boston: High-Tech, High Rises, and the Ted Williams Tunnel

Sometimes it seems as if everybody in Boston is carrying a laptop computer. With so many schools and colleges, it's not surprising that the city is a magnet for high-tech professionals. Boston has also accumulated some shiny new skyscrapers. In the late twentieth century, technology and construction came together to carry out one of the biggest **urban renewal** projects in the history of the United States. However, you can't even see most of it.

Why not? Because a lot of the work was done underground. The Big Dig replaced the old highway overpasses that had cut off the North End from downtown. It created a third tunnel to route traffic under Boston Harbor in addition to the Sumner Tunnel, completed in 1934, and the Callahan Tunnel, completed in 1961. Named after Boston Red Sox Hall of Fame hitter Ted Williams, the new tunnel is 8,448 feet long (that's 1.6 miles!). As of 2009, it was the longest road tunnel in the United States.

What do you see when you look at the Big Dig? Trees, fountains, and lots of people enjoying the Greenway, a park that stretches along Boston's waterfront, the newest link in the Emerald Necklace of one of America's oldest cities.

Did You Know?

Play Ball!

Built in 1912, Fenway Park, the home of the Boston Red Sox, is the oldest Major League Baseball stadium in the United States. Thousands of fans show up every April for opening day.

BOSTON

The steeple of the Old North Church houses the oldest church bells in North America. The eight bells range from three to twenty-four pounds. All can be rung by hand.
Top right: *Gelato*

Chapter

3

The Hub: Take a Whirl Around Boston

Bostonians call their city The Hub because it seems to be the center of so many things. All year, Boston is busy with festivals and events. Each neighborhood has its own feasts and flavors.

Boston has nearly twenty different neighborhoods. (Some are small areas in larger neighborhoods, so it depends on how you count.) There are four that people visit most often: the North End, Beacon Hill, Back Bay, and Chinatown. As you walk around them, you may see a few surprises, including swan boats, stone lions, and secret gardens.

The North End: Paul Revere and Pizza

The North End is Boston's first and oldest neighborhood. Every year, visitors from all over the world follow the Freedom Trail to Paul Revere's house and the Old North Church. It's also Boston's Italian neighborhood. People sit in outdoor cafés eating gelato (jeh-LAH-toh), which is Italian ice cream. They watch men

Cruising around the pond in the Public Garden on a Swan Boat is a fun summer treat. You can watch real swans swimming by, too.

playing bocce (BOT-chee), a game similar to bowling, in small parks. In August, the whole neighborhood turns out for St. Anthony's Feast, a celebration of the community's patron saint, complete with parades, bands, and all the food you can eat.

Beacon Hill: Brahmins and Secret Gardens

Years ago, Beacon Hill was home to some of Boston's most important families. People called them Brahmins because they formed such a select society. If you love gardens, visit Beacon Hill in the spring, when the neighborhood association gives a tour of the hidden gardens tucked behind the townhouses. At the top of the hill stands the Massachusetts State House, with its unmistakable copper-covered dome.

Some very lucky visitors to Boston get to go directly to jail. Why? The Charles Street Jail, a huge stone building at the bottom of Beacon Hill, was renovated and turned into an exclusive hotel in 2006. The rooms are very elegant, offering views of the Charles River and nearby Cambridge. Now, of course, you can leave whenever you like.

The Massachusetts State House was designed by Charles Bulfinch (1763–1844). America's first native-born professional architect, Bulfinch also helped restore Washington's Capitol building after the British burned it during the War of 1812.

Founded in 1884, the Boston Pops has had only three conductors in its entire history. One of them was John Williams, who also composed music for such popular movies as *Star Wars*, *Superman*, and *Raiders of the Lost Ark*. Keith Lockhart took over for Williams in 2003.

Back Bay: Fire and Ice!

As you stroll down Back Bay's wide streets lined with stately townhouses, it's hard to believe that all this land used to be underwater. When Boston was founded, Back Bay was part of the Charles River. Starting in 1857, city workers carted soil from the top of Beacon Hill to fill the bay and create more ground for the growing city. Today, Back Bay is home to the Boston Public Library, Trinity Church, and many art galleries along Newbury Street. It also hosts some of Boston's most popular festivals throughout the year.

Every July Fourth, thousands of people gather at the Charles River Esplanade (ES-pluh-nod) to celebrate Independence Day with a concert by the Boston Pops **orchestra** (OR-kes-truh) and a spectacular display of fireworks. Winters in Boston can be very cold, with temperatures plunging below freezing. But that won't stop Bostonians from coming out on New Year's Eve to admire the fancy ice sculptures in Copley Square and cheer Boston's First Night Parade as it marches down Boylston Street to the Common.

Chinatown: Lion Dances and Dim Sum
Pass through the big *paifang* on Beach Street and you'll find yourself surrounded by New England's best Chinese restaurants and outdoor markets. *Paifang* means "archway" in Chinese, and this one has a fierce-looking stone lion on either side. The lion stands for strength and protection. Every winter, residents welcome the Chinese New Year with lion dances and firecrackers. Summer brings the August Moon Festival, with more lion dances and sweet, round moon cakes.

On Sundays, families, both Asian and non-Asian, go to Chinatown for a brunch of tiny, delicious snacks called *dim sum*. When the weather is nice, you can visit Chinatown's new park along the Greenway and watch people concentrating on games of *Xian Qi* (pronounced *shiang-chi*), a form of Chinese chess.

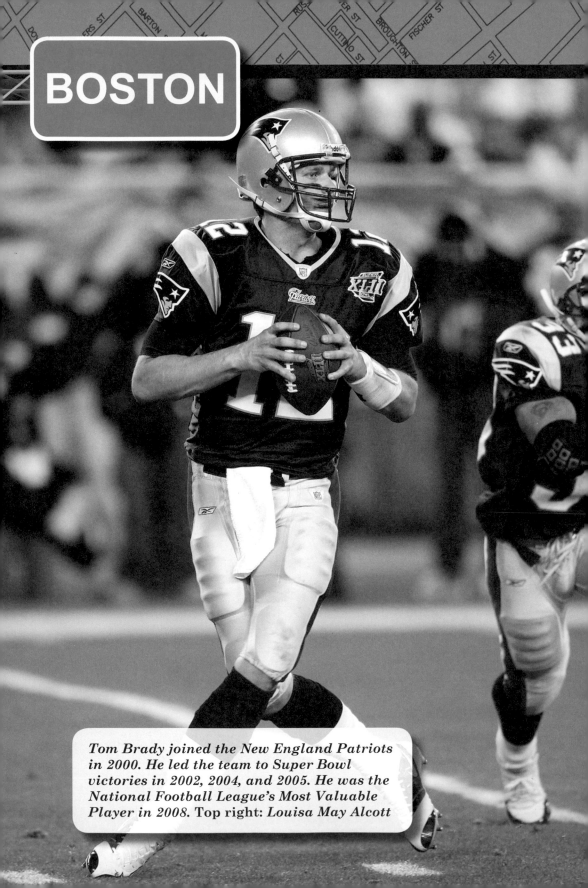

BOSTON

Tom Brady joined the New England Patriots in 2000. He led the team to Super Bowl victories in 2002, 2004, and 2005. He was the National Football League's Most Valuable Player in 2008. Top right: Louisa May Alcott

Poets, Scientists, and Politicians: Meet the People of Boston

Greater Boston has always been known for its writers, including Henry David Thoreau, author of *Walden*. He and his friend, the philosopher (fih-LAH-suh-fer) Ralph Waldo Emerson, lived near Boston from the 1830s through the 1860s. So did Louisa May Alcott, who wrote many books for children. One of them was *Little Women*, which was based on her own childhood in Concord, Massachusetts. Medicine and scientific research also keep a lot of Bostonians busy. The city has several top-notch hospitals, including Children's Hospital and Massachusetts General. At Brigham and Women's Hospital, Dr. Joseph Murray performed the first successful human organ transplant in 1954.

Boston's government consists of a mayor and city council. Political campaigns can get pretty feisty, but after the election everybody tries to get along.

Some of Boston's most famous citizens were born there. Others came from different states and countries.

Chapter 4

But they are all Bostonians. Here are three people whom Boston is proud to call its own.

Phillis Wheatley, Poet (1753–1784)

Born in Gambia, Africa, Phillis Wheatley was the first published African American poet in the United States. She came to Boston as a slave and served the Wheatley family, who taught her how to read and write. After the success of her first book of poems in 1773, the Wheatleys **emancipated** (ee-MAN-sih-pay-ted) her, and she traveled throughout New England and Europe. Today, a statue honoring her is located on Boston's Commonwealth Avenue.

Alexander Graham Bell, Scientist and Inventor (1847–1922)

Born in Scotland, Bell moved to Boston in 1871. He taught at Boston University and set up a laboratory to experiment with ways electricity might transmit sound. On March 10, 1876, he spilled some acid and called for his assistant, *Alexander Graham Bell* Thomas Watson, to help him. Watson heard his voice from a wire running between their rooms—the first "telephone call" in history. Today, Boston University offers an engineering scholarship in Bell's memory.

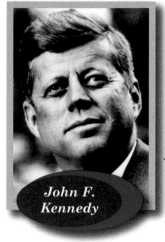

John F. Kennedy

John Fitzgerald Kennedy, U.S. President (1917–1963)

Born in Brookline, Massachusetts, less than a mile from Boston, John F. Kennedy attended Harvard University. During World War II, He joined the U.S. Navy. He received the Congressional (kun-GREH-shuh-nul) Medal of Honor for saving his crew after his boat, the PT109, went down. He became a U.S. senator from Massachusetts in 1953. In 1960, he was elected the 35th president of the United States. While in office he founded the Peace Corps and introduced new civil rights bills. On November 22, 1963, he was **assassinated** (uh-SAA-sih-nay-ted) in Dallas, Texas. Today, the John F. Kennedy Presidential Library and Museum, located on Boston Harbor, honors his legacy with the annual Profiles in Courage Essay Contest, open to high school students nationwide.

Did You Know?

In 1998, Bostonians Matt Damon and Ben Affleck won an Academy Award for the screenplay of *Good Will Hunting*, a movie about a math genius set in Boston and Cambridge. Damon also won the Academy Award for Best Actor for his role in the movie.

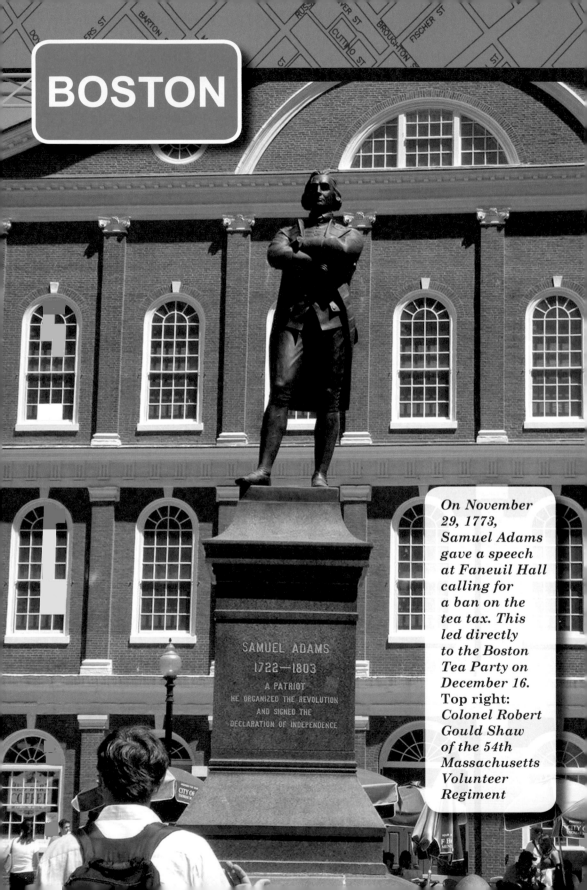

BOSTON

SAMUEL ADAMS
1722—1803
A PATRIOT
HE ORGANIZED THE REVOLUTION
AND SIGNED THE
DECLARATION OF INDEPENDENCE

On November 29, 1773, Samuel Adams gave a speech at Faneuil Hall calling for a ban on the tea tax. This led directly to the Boston Tea Party on December 16. Top right: Colonel Robert Gould Shaw of the 54th Massachusetts Volunteer Regiment

Chapter

Boston, Here We Come! Our Class Trip to Boston

After we learned a little more about Boston, we were finally ready for our class trip. We decided that we'd spend the morning following the Freedom Trail to see a few of the most important historic and Revolutionary War sites. Then we'd eat lunch at Faneuil Hall Marketplace, and finish our day with a ferry ride across the harbor to the Charlestown Navy Yard, where we'd take a guided tour of Old Ironsides.

The Freedom Trail starts at Boston Common and is marked with a red line on the walkway. Our first stop was the Massachusetts State House. We saw the Great Hall and took a peek at the House of Representatives and Senate Chambers, where the laws are made. Outside the State House, we checked out the memorial to the 54th Massachusetts Volunteer Regiment of African-American Civil War soldiers.

Two of the most famous sites on the Freedom Trail are the Old South Meeting House on Washington Street, where the Boston Tea Party started, and the

Paul Revere based his engraving of the Boston Massacre on a drawing by Boston artist Henry Pelham. His engraving does not show that the mob had been assaulting the troops before the British opened fire.

site of the Boston Massacre, a square outside the Old State House at the corner of Washington and State Streets. There, British troops fired on angry colonists, killing five of them on March 5, 1770.

The Old State House is now the home of the Bostonian Society. We stepped inside to see some cool exhibits about the city. After that, we headed across the street to Faneuil Hall.

Built in 1742, Faneuil Hall is a "town hall" to both Boston and the nation. Throughout the year, the hall hosts lectures and debates on politics, education, and other important issues.

The second floor of Faneuil Hall is known as the Great Hall. Between seven and twelve thousand immigrants become new citizens there every year.

Following the Freedom Trail through North End, we arrived at Paul Revere's house and the Old North Church, where the signal lanterns warning him of the British advance were hung from the steeple.

By noon we were glad to get back to Faneuil Hall and the nearby Marketplace for lunch. I couldn't decide between baked beans and clam chowder. I had a cup of each, followed by a scoop of maple walnut ice cream!

Ship ahoy! We boarded the ferry to the Charlestown Navy Yard at Long Wharf, and ten minutes later we were at the home of Old Ironsides. In the USS Constitution Museum, we had a few lessons in tying sailor's knots, reading navigational charts, using signal flags,

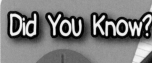

The grasshopper weathervane atop Faneuil Hall is made of copper and gilded with a thin layer of gold. It is 52 inches long and weighs 80 pounds. It has glass doorknobs for eyes and a stomach filled with colonial-era gold coins! It was "vane-napped" in 1974, but was returned and restored a few months later.

Paul Revere's House

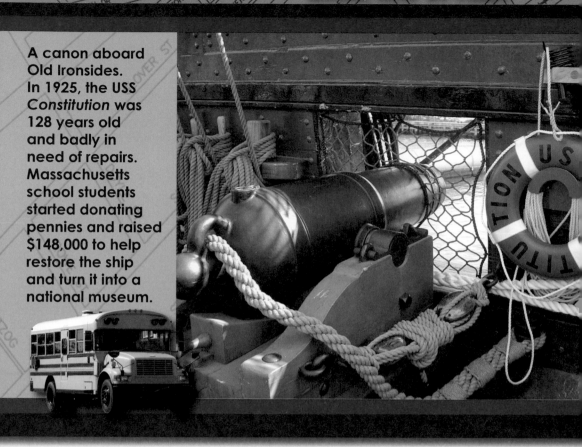

A canon aboard Old Ironsides. In 1925, the USS *Constitution* was 128 years old and badly in need of repairs. Massachusetts school students started donating pennies and raised $148,000 to help restore the ship and turn it into a national museum.

and, yes, swabbing the deck. Whew! Sailors sure kept busy!

On board the *Constitution* itself, we got a special tour from a real U.S. Naval Ensign, who took us through the ship from stem to stern—which means from front to back and everywhere in between.

We had a little extra time, so we went aboard the USS *Cassin Young*, a World War II destroyer, where we heard stories recorded by the men who served on her during the Battle of Okinawa in 1945.

We had an exciting day, and we had plenty to talk about on the way home. And guess what? My classmates unanimously elected me chairperson of next year's Fifth Grade Class Trip to Boston Committee! We've already made a new list of everything we all agree we absolutely have to see.

SCHOOL BUS TURN AHEAD

Just The Facts

Founded: 1630

Location: Massachusetts

Form of Government: Mayor and elected city council

Population: 599,350*

Percent of Population Under 18: 20%

U.S. Rank: 24th most populous city

Density: Approximately 12,350 people per square mile

Size: 48 square miles of land. City limits also include 41.2 square miles of water (in Boston Harbor)

Average Elevation: 19 feet above sea level

Highest Point: Bellevue Hill, 330 feet above sea level

Lowest Point: Sea level

Average Temperature: 43°F**

Average High: 53°F

Average Low: 44°F

Hottest Month: July, 74°F average

Coldest Month: January, 28°F average

Average Annual Precipitation: 43 inches

Major Industries: Education, banking, insurance, health care, technology, and research

Number of Public Schools: 143

Major Neighborhoods: Allston-Brighton, Back Bay, Beacon Hill, Charlestown, Chinatown, Dorchester, East Boston, Jamaica Plain, the North End, Roxbury, South Boston, the South End

Public Parks: Approximately 2,260 acres of city-owned land, including Boston Common, the Public Garden, the Fenway, the Charles River Esplanade, Franklin Park, and the Greenway

Public Transportation: Massachusetts Bay Transportation Authority (MBTA) subway, bus, commuter rail, and ferries

Major Sports Teams: Boston Red Sox—Baseball; Boston Celtics—Basketball; Boston Bruins—Hockey; New England Patriots—Football

Major Museums and Cultural Centers: Museum of Fine Arts, Isabella Stewart Gardner Museum, Boston Children's Museum, Museum of Science, Boston Aquarium, Symphony Hall, and Franklin Park Zoo

*All population statistics, City of Boston 2007 Census
**All weather statistics, U.S. National Weather Service, 2007

Thar' She Blows!

Make a Sailor's Windsock

Boston has always been a sailing city, and knowing which way the wind blows is important to sailors. All along Boston's waterfront, brightly colored windsocks catch the breeze. A simple windsock can be made from a cardboard cylinder and lots of ribbons.

What You Need:

A sturdy cardboard cylinder (such as an oatmeal container or a round ice-cream carton)

Sharp scissors

Brightly colored paper to cover the cylinder (I like to use an old map because it makes me think of traveling. You may want to use wrapping paper, the Sunday comics, or construction paper.)

Good quality glue

Stickers or glitter (optional)

A hole-punch strong enough to punch through cardboard

Two pieces of string about 4 feet long, and one short piece about six inches long

Lots of ribbons, each about 3 feet long

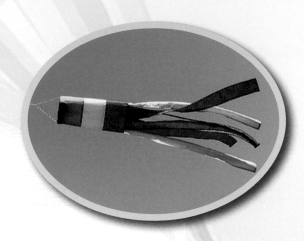

What You Do:

1 Remove the top and cut the bottom off your cylinder. It should be open at both ends. Make sure it is clean and dry.

2 Cut your chosen paper to fit around the outside of the cylinder.

3 Glue the paper to the cylinder.

4 Decorate the cylinder with construction paper cutouts, stickers, or glitter if you like.

5 Punch four evenly spaced holes around the top edge.

6 Run the two 4-foot lengths of string through the holes to make two long loops that cross at the top.

7 Tie these loops together at the top with the 6-inch piece of string, and make a small loop so that you will have a hook for hanging your windsock.

8 Glue one end of a ribbon to the inside of the other end of the cylinder. Make sure the rest of the ribbon can float free. Repeat until the bottom of the cylinder has a complete circle of ribbon streamers.

Now you have a windsock. Hang it from the porch or a tree or in an open window on a sunny day and watch which way the wind blows!

Boston Historical Timeline

1630 Puritan colonists from England establish the town of Boston.

1635 Boston Latin School for Boys, the first public school in the United States, opens its doors.

1636 Harvard University, the first university in the United States, opens in Cambridge, Massachusetts, across the Charles River from Boston.

1742 Faneuil Hall, Boston's first public meeting hall, is built. It swiftly becomes a central location for Bostonians protesting British rule.

1770 On March 5, a mob of angry colonists confronts British soldiers. The soldiers fire, killing five in what will be called the Boston Massacre.

1773 On December 16, a group of Boston men board English ships and throw boxes of tea into the harbor to protest English taxes upon the colonies; the event is called the Boston Tea Party.

1775 On April 19, Paul Revere rides from Boston's North End to the towns of Lexington and Concord to warn the residents that British troops are advancing from Boston. The first battle of the Revolutionary War is fought at Lexington. On June 17, British troops seize the American fort in Charlestown in the Battle of Bunker Hill.

1776 On March 17, called Evacuation Day, all British troops surrender, departing by ship from Boston Harbor.

1783 Slavery is declared illegal in Massachusetts. Quock Walker, a slave in the town of Barre, Massachusetts, sues for his freedom and carries his case all the way to the State Supreme Judicial Court. The court rules in his favor, declaring that slavery is not legal according to the state constitution of 1780. On September 3, the Treaty of Paris officially ends the Revolutionary War.

1797 The USS *Constitution*, one of the U.S. Navy's first commissioned ships, is constructed in Boston's shipyard.

1800 Charlestown Navy Yard is established by the U.S. Navy.

1820s Irish immigrants begin to arrive in Boston. By the end of the nineteenth century, they will have become Boston's largest ethnic group.

1822 Boston is officially incorporated as a city.

1831 William Lloyd Garrison founds *The Liberator*, the most famous antislavery newspaper in the United States.

1837 The Public Garden, a beloved park, is laid out across Charles Street from Boston Common.

1848 Boston Public Library, the first public library in the United States, is established by city charter. It will open in 1854. In 1895, the library will move to Copley Square.

1857 Boston starts to fill in the bay on the south side of the Charles River to create more land for the growing city. The area will come to be known as Back Bay.

1863 The 54th Massachusetts Infantry Regiment of the Union Army, the first African American regiment of the Civil War, assembles under the leadership of Colonel Robert Gould Shaw.

1866 The American Equal Rights Association, an organization promoting voting rights for women, holds its first national meeting in Boston.

1872 On November 9, a massive fire destroys most of downtown Boston, including many buildings from the early colonial era. John Damrell, Boston's fire chief, will become one of the first activists to call for a national fire prevention and building code.

1876 Alexander Graham Bell, an immigrant from Scotland, invents the telephone in his Boston laboratory.

1878–1900 Boston's Emerald Necklace, a series of parks stretching across the city, is built under the planning and supervision of landscape architect Frederick Law Olmsted.

1897 The Tremont Street Subway, the first underground city rail system in the United States, opens in Boston.

1912 Fenway Park, home of the Boston Red Sox, opens in the Kenmore Square neighborhood.

1919 On January 15, a tank holding 2.3 million gallons of molasses bursts, flooding North End and claiming 21 lives.

1941–1945 During World War II, over 50,000 civilian workers build ships in the Charlestown Navy Yard.

1954 Dr. Joseph Murray performs the world's first successful kidney transplant at Boston's Peter Bent Brigham Hospital (now called Brigham and Women's Hospital).

1991 Boston begins a construction project to lower the elevated cross-town highway called the central artery and route traffic through a series of new tunnels. Known as the Big Dig, this is one of the largest city projects in U.S. history.

2003 Part of the Big Dig is completed. The Greenway, a public park, stretches along the waterfront where the elevated artery used to run.

2004 The Boston Red Sox win their first World Series since 1918.

2007 The Mashpee Wampanoag tribe, the first group of Native Americans to greet the Puritans as they arrived in Boston in 1630, receives official tribal recognition from the U.S. Department of the Interior.

2009 Governor Duval Patrick declares February 29 "Massachusetts Day of the Frog." It honors the efforts of biologists at the Franklin Park Zoo who are saving endangered species of frogs throughout the world.

Glossary

abolitionist (aa-buh-LIH-shuh-nist)—Someone opposed to slavery. Boston was home to many abolitionists during the years before the Civil War.

assassinated (uh-SAA-sih-nay-ted)—Killed for political reasons.

Beantown—A nickname given to Boston because Bostonians were said to eat so many baked beans. The beans, made with molasses and pork fat, were a cheap and nutritious supper during colonial days.

common (as in *grazing common*)—An area of a town that was set aside for grazing sheep and cattle during colonial days. Today, Boston Common is a popular public park.

emancipate (ee-MAN-sih-payt)—To set free. Massachusetts officially ended slavery in 1783, eighty years before Abraham Lincoln's Emancipation Proclamation freed the slaves nationally.

immigrants (IH-mih-grints)—People who move into a country from another country.

militia (mih-LIH-shuh)—A volunteer military force that is not part of the regular army, but may aid the regular army in times of danger. During the Revolutionary War, many towns and cities sent militias to aid General George Washington's Continental Army.

Minutemen (MIH-nit-men)—A nickname given to the New England militia volunteers because they claimed they could be ready to fight at a minute's notice.

orchestra (OR-kes-truh)—A group of musicians playing a variety of instruments who perform together. Boston has two well-known orchestras—the Boston Symphony Orchestra, which plays at Symphony Hall during the winter, and the Boston Pops, which performs during the summer.

peninsula (peh-NIN-suh-luh)—A body of land bordered by water on three sides.

Puritans (PYOOR-ih-tins)—A group of English Protestants (Christians who did not agree with the Catholic Church) who arrived in Massachusetts in 1630.

ropewalk—A long, narrow factory building in which hemp fibers were twisted into rope either by hand or by steam-powered engines.

Shawmut—The original name given by the Wampanoag people to the area now called Boston.

statistics (stuh-TIS-tiks)—Pieces of data or types of measures. Population, land area, and average weather temperature are all statistics.

triple-decker—A three-story house, usually made of wood, with a separate apartment on each floor.

urban renewal—Construction to redesign and improve a city.

Wampanoag (wom-puh-NOH-ug)—A Native American tribe from southeastern New England.

Further Reading

Books

Barter, James. *A Travel Guide to Colonial Boston*. San Diego, California: Lucent Books, 2004.

Berger, Melvin. *Did You Invent the Phone, Mr. Bell?* New York: Scholastic, 2007.

Harper, Judith. *John F. Kennedy: Our Thirty-Fifth President*. Chanhassen, Minnesota: Child's World, 2002.

Krensky, Stephen. *What's the Big Idea?: Four Centuries of Innovation in Boston*. Watertown, Massachusetts: Charlesbridge, 2008.

Lasky, Kathryn. *A Voice of Her Own: The Story of Phillis Wheatley, Slave Poet*. Cambridge, Massachusetts: Candlewick Press, 2003.

Longfellow, Henry Wadsworth, and Christopher Bing, illustrator. *The Midnight Ride of Paul Revere*. Brooklyn, New York: Handprint Books, 2001.

Vanderwalker, Peter. *The Big Dig: Reshaping an American City*. Boston, Massachusetts: Little, Brown and Co., 2001.

Weitman, Jacqueline Preiss. *You Can't Take a Balloon into the Museum of Fine Arts*. New York: Dial Books, 2002.

Wilson, Deirdre. *The Lobster Kids Guide to Exploring Boston: 12 Months of Fun*. Montreal: Lobster Press, 2001.

PHOTO CREDITS: Cover—p. II—U.S. Navy; p. 19—John Singer Sargent; p. 20—Howard R. Hollem; p. 28—Paul Spinelli, Getty Images; p. 34—Paul Revere; all other photos—Barbara Marvis. Every effort has been made to locate all copyright holders of material used in this book. If any errors or omissions have occurred, corrections will be made in future editions of the book.

Further Reading

Works Consulted

Clark, Edward. *Black Writers in New England*. Boston: National Park Service, 1985.

Felton, Robert Todd. *Walking Boston: 34 Tours through Beantown's Cobblestone Streets, Historical Districts, Ivory Towers, and New Waterfront*. Berkeley, California: Wilderness Press, 2008.

Fisher, Chris. *Birds of Boston*. Renton, Washington: Lone Pine Press, 1993.

Hanson, Mitchell. *A Paradise of All These Parts: A Natural History of Boston*. Boston: Beacon Press, 2008.

Handlin, Oscar. *Boston's Immigrants, 1790–1880*. Cambridge, Massachusetts: Harvard University Press, 1959.

Kay, Jane Holtz. *Lost Boston*. Boston: Houghton Mifflin, 1980.

O'Connor, Thomas. *Eminent Bostonians*. Cambridge, Massachusetts: Harvard University Press, 2002

———. *The Hub: Boston Past and Present*. Boston: Northeastern University Press, 2001.

Rogers, Alan. *Boston, City on a Hill: An Illustrated History*. Sun Valley, California: American Historical Press, 2007.

Seasholes, Nancy. *Gaining Ground: A History of Landmaking in Boston*. Cambridge, Massachusetts: MIT Press, 2003.

Taylor, Karen Cord. *Blue Laws, Brahmins, and Breakdown Lands: An Alphabetic Guide to Boston and Bostonians*. Chester, Connecticut: Globe Pequot Press, 1989.

Whitehill, Walter Muir. *Boston: A Topographical History*. Cambridge, Massachusetts: Harvard University Press, 1968.

Wilson, Susan. *Boston Sights and Insights: An Essential Guide to Historic Landmarks In and Around Boston*. Boston: Beacon Press, 2003.

Zaitzevsky, Cynthia. *Frederick Law Olmsted and the Boston Parks System*. Cambridge, Massachusetts: Harvard University Press, 1982.

On the Internet

Boston Black Heritage Trail: Museum of African American History
http://www.afroammuseum.org/trail.htm

The Boston Historical Society
http://www.bostonhistory.org

Boston National Historic Park; National Historic Park Service, U.S. Deptartment of the Interior http://www.nps.gov/bost

City of Boston Official Website
http://www.cityofboston.gov

Faneuil Hall Marketplace: Gateway to the City
http://www.faneuilhallmarketplace.com

The USS Constitution Museum
http://www.ussconstitutionmuseum.org

Index

ABOUT THE AUTHOR

A former history major, Patrice Sherman is especially interested in social and cultural history. She is the author of the picture books *The Sun's Daughter* and *Ben and the Proclamation of Emancipation*. Her articles have been published in *Learning Through History* magazine, and she produced *Growing Up at Work: A History of Child Labor in America,* a multimedia educational program for the Massachusetts History Workshop. Sherman has lived in Cambridge, Massachusetts—right across the Charles River from Boston—since 2000. Before that, she lived in Boston for over twenty years. In her spare time, she likes to go to Boston to visit its many museums, the public library in Copley Square, and Goodspeed's used bookstore, which is over a hundred years old.